The Door Left Open

And other poems…

by

Nicholas Damion Alexander

ISBN: 978-81-19654-59-8

First Edition: 2023
Rs. 200/-

Cyberwit.net
HIG 45 Kaushambi Kunj, Kalindipuram
Allahabad - 211011 (U.P.) India
http://www.cyberwit.net
Tel: +(91) 9415091004
E-mail: info@cyberwit.net

Printed at Repro India Limited.

Dedicated to my father Maurice Ignatius Alexander AKA Esau/Zippy and fellow poet Colin St. Leger Lewis. May their beautiful souls rest in power.

Contents

The door left open

There is only the slightest evidence
That air exists outside my window
That stuff of the universe
Anaximenes named Reality:
A microscopic shifting of the leaves
On a not-too-large breadfruit tree;
Its once evergreen leaves now brown with rust
And sprinkled with yellow stains.

Civilization has long died here.
Parasitic plants lurch along a rotting fence
As a glare of light appears slanted
As in an impressionist painting.

Then, without warning, the air lifts;
Languid leaves dance like bacchanal
Fast approaching. Lecherous lizards lurk.
Light engulfs space,
The tactile taste of rain whets
The appetite of insects scouring a yard
Indicative of a meandering mind.

Mortal Wound (for Miss Mighty)

She bled in silence
From behind her wooden office desk
Beside me, as stiff as death,
Unflinching like the grave.
The gaping wound hid
From mortal sight,
A pretense of joy
Given to the worrisome world.

And though I tried
To heal her open wound
With friendship and adoration,
The bandage would not stick
Without her own removal
Of the scars time marked
Her soft flesh with.

Sometimes a name's just a name
And there's nothing 'Mighty'
About the timid hiding
Their mortal wounds with work,
Bleeding in silence,
A pretense of joy
On their long but beautiful faces.

The stuff of poetry

This is the stuff of poetry:
Smooth breeze, straggling fence, with green yellow
Leaves shimmying in the day's sunlight.

Winds mount like hikers
On the Blue Mountain trail, a scene
I know all too well: the late evening journey
To Mavis Bank by bus, usually a small one
Ransacked with hikers and townsfolk alike.
Then the arrival at the riverbed;
But not before a long walk down a great slope of hill.

The raging river gapes like mouths
Yearning for the fit food of feet
Determined that a little wetness
Is nothing compared to the glory
At the end of this sweating trek.

Silence now. Only the sweet sound
Of wind forcing its way through leaves
Tightly packed together-hikers
Skipping over slippery stone heads,
Darting up a trail that leads
To a narrow path against the line
Of a mountain looming overhead
Like these trees outside my window.

The salt smell of rain
And the sound of liquid feet

Tip Toeing on the leaves outside
Recall the soaking experience
Of another journey when we tore
Through torrential weather en route
To the fiery presence of a God
Seated on His Throne in secret places
Like "Stand Pipe" and "Look Out".
Until we entered His Throne Room:
Portland Gap, somewhere in the Third Heaven
Of that Blue Mountain Peak.

Ironing Board

Carton boxes piled on top of each other
Struggle to survive the mess of a room
Where grips of clothes thrown to the opposite end
Sandwich an almost out of place ironing board
Neatly covered by a white towel
To tell the tale of women's place in men's lives.
Inside those boxes are all kinds of books
A man has read or intend to read-
Philosophy, religion, literature and such:
Descartes's Discourse on Method,
Dickens's A Tale of Two Cities,
Lying among the clothes left unattended
In the corner like the neglect of love,
Matrimony not thought of for some time,
Stained by the imprints of a policeman's promiscuity.
But that board stands with a distant wife's hope,
A woman living abroad,
Though covered in the white towel
Of a mistress's contumacy
And sweated upon by her omniscience,
Pressed down with the weight of us tenants.
It groans for the decrement of a wrinkled marriage
But at the same time reflects the love
Of women who balance the miserable life
Of a man too preoccupied with his own lust
To see what he is missing.

A long walk

The afternoon is full
Of varying themes:
Men drinking conch
Soup at a shop, surrounded
By feline and canine
Predators waiting
Under old wooden
Structures for something
To drop, just before
Opposing denominations
Fading behind the sound
Of Michael Jackson's
"Wanna be startin' somethin".
Four love-struck feet
Press their way
To truth, him feeling
The anguish
Of her impregnation;
She sensing
His flippant anxiety.
A male plethora of eyes
Watch her beauty,
Cunning feminine
Smiles tempt his commitment.
But they come and go
To and from
Where they were, breathing
Heavily from the long walk
To finally rest in a new bed
Full of old uncertainties.

Good Friday

Good Friday. A silent breeze infiltrates.
The sound of small leaves rattling
While larger ones dance
To a sudden surge of wavering wind.

It is late afternoon
Just prior spates of intense heat.
All day long the TV
Displays movies about Moses, Jesus,
David and Daniel while I lie
In bed reading
Descartes's Meditations
With a woeful woman by my side
Perusing classic literature. The day's
Uncanny brightness fades like faith
On this Good Friday devoid
Of its traditional darkness and gloom.

And as early evening approaches
Day deepens, winds mount like messiah
To his Cross, descends to the grave
As night trickles like the tears
Of the double-minded voices next
Door, praising God
While chatting people's business.

Comfort zones

A male child clings to his mother's bosom,
Sucking his thumb. The woman smiles at me
And a conversation soon develops.

Outside this public transport the sun smiles
To welcome the morning. Last night a child
Said in her usual frisky way,
"I love my daddy; I don't love you."

I smile the night to sleep
Seeing her in the morning spread-eagled
Over the bed like the sun spread-eagled
Over the sky, stationary in its own frisky way.

The morning sighs as the sun scampers
Behind dark clouds. Night is summoned,
The purr of an engine reiterates
A crooner's wooing words of love
As I sooth myself to sleep
With melancholy music.

Family Matters

Silence once more. A dim fluorescent light
Darkens the room as I watch its slight glow
From underneath this book of poems I read.
The woman next to me shouts at the child
Fondling the books left carelessly
On a makeshift bed.
"These are his prized possessions." She warns
As I remove myself
From this ready-made family.

The child is not mine. She knows it all
Too well, dancing on my torso
Whenever she's here-laughing and singing,
Crying and hoping that somehow this make-
Shift dad of a lighter hue might one day
Love her as her father does;
Love her as he loves her mother, planting
Kisses like the half-deaf man plants
Seeds in the yard, hoping for a spurt
Of rain that cares enough to water earth
With its tears-so one day we can reap its harvest.

The poet writes her pain

(1)

She lies prostrate on a new bed
Scattered with old newspapers
Worshiping her pain

Outside is wet
With early morning dew
Air is ice
Tranquilized by the slow sound
Of heaven's tears
Sprinkling leaves

The morning breaths
A sigh
As the poet writes her pain

(2)

Light exists
Somewhere outside this bleak room
Somewhere beyond the white sky
Of a morning writhing
In her pain.

The embodiment of fear

That afternoon the sky
Was troubled with fear's
Bright glow; the sun firing
Bullets of light beams to an earth
Swollen with panic
As its inhabitants
Shot their way home
From work, school or play.

One among them was about
To go: the hand of death
Clutched him by the collar
After he clutched a woman's bag.
He reached in turn
For his criminal defense.
But bang! The day slept, earth
Sinking like bullets
In their target; a stream
Of blood settled to the ground.

The sky wailed
With the embodiment
Of fear, the sun blowing
Away the smoke
From the cop's gun, but not
The smell of death.

Sick Bay

The constant wailing
Of tongues down the aisle
In this cacophony
Of voices embalms;
Reverences my mind
To a sermon of sounds
Playing on the heart
Like drum beats
In a deliverance session.
Spirit-drunk dances
Of the sick prance on
In this healing hall.

Old world, new sounds

(for Lorna Goodison)

Under the calm sky of early evening
Before an audience of attentive locals,
You spoke of the drums beating in a circle
In an attempt to build a rhythmic center
In a faraway abode where bush medicine rules
And a new science as old as time heals.

The new reggae sounds
Of an old African world lingered
In the background of this your home
Made into a distant place you visit now
Ever so often, disrupted your delivery,
Ignoring your old craft
For new rhythms of tones that pulse
In the present, spiral in the sky
Like African locusts,
Disrupting the calm sky
While you spoke of the drums
Beating in a circle.

First Job

After nearly quarter-a-century of life
I found my funeral downtown
In a lane called Camperdown Road.

There was a loud cheer
When my name was announced
At the first general assembly,
Almost like the weeping of relatives
At a thanksgiving service-or the cheers
For an athlete dying young:
The demented irony of listening
To mourners at one's casket,
Feeling the sigh of regret
From those who failed to reconcile
Differences; hearing the labored breathing
Of the sincere-the hypocritical tears
Of the religious who are not sure if God
Was on your side.
That's what it was like
That day when, at twenty five, I got
My first teaching job
That marked my new life's beginning.

Anxiety Attack

A proud prostitute skitters across the road,
A mere silhouette in the darkest night;
Her tight little shorts is passion's color,
That much I can see in the shifting shadow's light.

The woman lying in my arms is sick,
Diagnosed with anxiety attack;
She fell at ten twenty five in a night
When malice howled like night dogs in a pack,

Roaming the road at this ungodly hour.
The howls of clandestine lust resonate
Through the sin-stained pre-dawn air.
Yet I'm happy to have overcome hate.

Now arming love in a cab, clutching its breath,
Feeling the power of life rise in its breasts
Is an anxiety attack I'd have
Forever like dogs howling midnight in my chest.

Growing Library

Those three bookshelves contain Carter, Walcott,
Morris, Brown, Gray and other West Indian greats.

There is also Donne, Shakespeare, Marvell
And a number of classic English men

Who wrote in strict meter and end rhymes
Well-structured in sonnets, true to the form

Of conventional poetry. Then there
Is the break from convention with Whitman,

Eliot, Sexton and Dickinson to some extent.
Until the American Revolution starts

With Black Poetry: Hayden, Randall, Clarke,
Hughes and a splattering of female poetesses

Like Angelou, Walker, Sanchez
And Giovanni (Sexton too but she's white)

To complete the growing library of a man
Who himself, for twenty five years, loves to write.

Our Fortunate Mistake

On my usual early morning walk
I saw a house without veranda grills.

"An odd sight in this day and age."
I thought looking again to see grills

On the windows and around the door.
"Now that's more like it!" I proclaimed.

I recall twenty years or so ago,
Living uptown(as I do now) in a house

Without grills(though there were grills
On the windows): we'd often leave

The doors unlocked through the night;
Waking up the next morning to discover

Our fortunate mistake. But one night, Boogie,
My mother's red-haired cousin rode his luck too far

When, while watching TV late that night,
He left the door wide open, inviting

Two unwelcomed guests with shiny black
Objects in their hands that they used to target fear.

A man's unfaithfulness

Beside a towering three-storied building
A thorny tree dances in the wind
Just before a frail fence braced by a coop
And a burnt-blue bin. Pretty red flowers
Decorate the otherwise dour scene
Where larger trees hide a horrid house
Burnt by a man's unfaithfulness.

Today the house is abandoned
As if haunted, its inside hollow.
The outer walls dark like the sin
That formed its ruin. But the man
Still lurks under a gazebo nearby,
Deep in thought, tormented, as if thinking
Of the woman who once lived
With him for nearly quarter of a century;
Who helped him to build
This little castle of a cottage
He destroyed with derelict desire.

Market day's End

I press by vendors selling fish, beef, pork,
And all types of seasonings to spice the pot
Of those who roam the crowded walkways
Of Downtown, Kingston in search
Of affordable condiments to sustain their lives.

Flies fester like cancer, dogs scour
Like plague, the air rancid with the frank smell
Of market day's end. I plod past the pressing crowd
Fermenting in the orange gloss
Of mid-evening's singe of sunset,
Weed petrifying the air to a fossil.

The day hardens like stone,
The wrinkled sky signaling time's ruin;
The stench of overnight meat steaming sensuously
Into the next day as I make my way home
From the place where so many compress their needs
To save a buck or two.

River tale (for Bilton Bryan)

He told the story of how,
As Pre-Independence kids
Living in the country,
They'd go down to the river
To fish. But it wasn't always easy
Because, sometimes, those gloss-eyed
Creatures hovering under the deep dark
Waters shaded by an enormous mango tree,
Seemed to know their intent
And would hide themselves under the murky depths.

But it wasn't until his elder half-brother
Came one day with his spear
And plunged into that mystery world below
That he realized his own fear
And compulsion for life's dark secrets:
God and Devil, angels and demons.

And so, in time, he found himself
Plunging into the desire
Of that world below, wanting never
To come up for breath;
Instead to revel in the green-deep glory of God
While struggling against the temptation of the devil.

Nine Night

It was not like other nine nights
Though they served us mannish water.

There was no one seated around
A veranda talking of days past
And those to come. Old folks
Were not in abundance, watching
The young sink in a corner of the yard,
They themselves watching the elders
Talk of life and death.

Instead there was this big sound box
And a selector shouting, "Nuh linga,
Do di gully creepa!". Young people
Followed cue, doing the latest moves
Under the concealing light of the moon
Out in the open air with no elders
"In attendance" , watching Mento, Poco
And Quadrill syncretize with North America.

But the ancestors were there
Where Africa and The New World
Found a common ground
In which to express themselves
Through modern music.

Revelers' All

The crowd pressed dryly against each other
With embracing familiarity,
Sweat threading through the humidity
In this closely-knitted cloth of brothers
And sisters swaying to the soca
And reggae rhythms of a Kingston carnival:
The sweet body action of revelers all
In one motion, causing the hot air to shudder.

Torsos gyrated, hands flew madly
About, some with a singular intent;
Heads bobbed, feet pranced, faces smiling gladly
As arms lurched, knees knocked with backs bent,
Concealing hands searching the pocket of one
Who was soon to be disheartened by fun
Upon discovery of a stolen wallet.

Carnival '09

Dance di soca
Dance di soca
Like a
Fire
In yu belly
Mix it with di
Mix it with di
Reggae reggae
Feel di rhythm
Feel di rhythm
Hit yu wid no
Wid no
Pain
Play the game
Of love
Of life
Feel di breath
Reenergize
Afta yu realize
Di soca, di reggae
Remain

Dance di soca
Dance di reggae
Like a fire
In yu belly
Mix it wid di pain
Of life, feel
Di rhythm

Of death
Feel the breath
Reenergize
When yu realize
Yuself.

Creation

Feet step
In unison with
The rhythm
Of the night
Like sweet serenade
Of sounds

Lingering in the ears
Of those who pose
A threat to danger

Under arching dome of thought

I
Hear the sound
Of muse
Sick awaken

Breath

god is deaf
Until the heart
Sings
god is deaf
Until the night
Cries

And I pen
A tune that dances

Red
On the white page

Of creation

Registration Day

This sea of maroon and brown bobs and weaves
Before my glittering eye, under the slope
Of a steel sky whose gray clouds reveal light
Peeping from its openings. I listen for
The break in rhythm, the swish of water
Splashing on rocks that create a phallic
Symbol in the mind. But all I hear is
The cackling of geese at this sea's dark shores.

No birds in sight nor rocks nor clouds, not even
The giant sea with its warring waves, shining
In the eye-only the presentation
Of a speech before a crowd of half-dead
Students listening to the disclosure;
Waiting for the ebb and tide to find them
Washed up on the shores of graduation.

Thank God it's Friday

(I)

The bus is late
Or maybe it is I
Who am late?

The morning stirs
Softly.
A dog on cue
At its Master's gate;
Not starving
In a Blakean state.
Rub-
Ber wheels dis-
Rupt the reticence
Of Fridays'
Sunrays
Pelting the as-
Phalted earth

A burnt out bus
Broadcasts
The thanksgiving
Of the living
God
Who burns Judgment
Down on sinners
In that final
Act of love.

(II)

A woman on the radio
Speaks politricks to the deaf ears
Of listeners promoting suffering
For survival, compromise for comfort.
But I listen with ears hardened
By truth; despite the soft crooning
Of good news stifled by a gush
Of artificial air. The silence of Fridays
Return and the gospel is spread
To the four corners of our world.
It is imperative: we must prove
Our martyrdom with suffering,
Our faith with foolhardiness
And die on buses salted by the smell
Of the same sea that surrounds our lives.

(III)

I return to the beach
Where the waves of the warring sea glitter in my eye;
To the solace that is
My anxiety. This sea
Doesn't hear my heart
Though it echoes inside
A shell of hollow dreams,
Thrown ashore by a thoughtless wave indifferent to memories.

(IV)

It is with this heavy heart
I return to the sea
Without being anywhere near the sea.

(V)

It is half-
Pass late evening
And finally
A bus to take
Me home
To my bed of discomfort.

A woe man's moods

1. " Morning"

Cold metal sounds,
A woman's lament
Bellows
Resonance
Of her aching stomach.

2. " Afternoon"

Silence.
Lazy leaves whisper
The secret of the ages
As she sleeps
In a bed
Of anguish.

3. " Night"

The anger of a man
Invades her peace
In a conflict
Of masculine clamor and
Feminine reticence.

Abode

At nights I slumber
Home to my crypt
And hang my soul
In a closet;

Then sleep in a bed of thorns,
Dreaming of the living
Until death comes
And wakes me in the mourning.

Ghetto sounds

Reggae is sweet ghetto sound
Like stinking stagnant gutter
Water streaming down the streets
Of Downtown, Kingston,
Children dancing in the streets
To its alluring aroma.

Ghetto phat women gyrate
To its pulsing beat,
The rhythm of African drums
In their hips.
Dread-
Locked men apparition
The weed's smoke;
Bopping to the side
Of the street, meditating
The lyrics, penetrating
The vibes, poeticizing
The atmosphere
With the fear
Of Babylon's wailing sirens.

Healing sounds

There is a Constant Spring
Flowing to Half-Way-Tree
From Stony Hill; flowing
With deep waters, purifying
Bitter waters, irrigating
The land of reggae:
A pandemic like plague;
A worldwide sound
Of waters flowing sweetly
Through houses
Made of cement, houses
Made of wood.

Coughs, sneezes,
Hog flu, recession
Healed. A nation
At the Cross
Roads, rev-
Elling to the heavy sounds
Of a system causing
Public disturbance.
Downtown drowning in
The roar of the reggae,
The reggae reveling
The joys of a people
Suffering, praising, hailing 'Father', drowning
Sorrows in the healing
Waters of a music
That has spread worldwide

Like pandemic
Soothing pain, rising
Like baptism of the believer
To a new life, devoid
Of old ignorance.

My Mother's Salt

(1)

My mother cooked with salt,
Flavoring our lives
With the spice of her choice…
A white grain from the sea
That added new worlds of taste
To children made of mixed spices

(2)

My father loved his pepper
Heating up her pot
With its red flames,
That little masculine bulb
Men use to show brav-
Ado about nothing.

(3)

We ate of Mother's salt
All our lives 'til we grew
Old enough to insist
She travel to the sea
Of her own spice, a-
Way from the red heat
Of our father's pepper.

(4)

Today, fifteen years on
My mother has stopped
Cooking with that spice
As white as my father's skin.
And we have grown accus-
Tomed to his hot spice,
Hardly remembering
Her love for little white grains
Drawn from the sea.

Heroes' Park

I walked through Heroes' Park
Passing men
Jogging, girls playing

With themselves; men
Playing with them-
Selves, trees swaying

In themselves

There were no He-
Roes there
Where everything was play-
Ing with themselves,
In themselves, for them-
Selves

And I was no differ-
Ent, a strange
Her voice sings
In my ears

Whenever I am near
The place where your face
Leaves its picture in my mind
And your quarrels are
My lullaby

Leaves me hanging, leaves me
Playing with myself,
For myself, in
My self

Home guards

From this enclosed window I observe
Menacing men and women stationed like home guards
Before signs marked "JLP"; at the entrance
Of a lane leading to nowhere.

Bars, shops line the parameters
Of a place so many call 'home',
"Family, father, sistren" are cries
That sweeten the air.

But in this box the air is cold.
Ice drips from faces frozen
With melancholia while the warm breath
Of those outsiders smear these window panes
With talks of religion and politricks,
Life and love, even death;
Trying hard to break the ice
Of living the cold, hard ghetto life.

Overhead fan

This fan breathing heavily above my head
Sounds like the sea

Rolling onto sandy shores, late in the after-
Noon when darkness approaches.

In this dim room I hear a young lady
Whisper something about sibling rivalry

And how she cannot get along with her sister
No matter how she tries.

Her voice breaks like the wind, breaking waves
Rolling into the shore, saying

"Relationships are meant to be broken"
Like heavy waves must be dissolved

By soft sand. And so I remove myself
From the shores of that room,

Where the waves of an overhead fan
Reminds me of my own sister,

Leaving my sunken footprints in the soft sand
As quiet as a whisper

Graveyard poet

"The poet is a gardener in a graveyard"
-George Elliott Clarke

Digging up malice
And discontentment

Planting words of hope
Sowing seeds of love

Over tombstones

Yet reaping harvests
Of pain and turmoil

Like a gardener's blistered hands

To be Jamaican

… Is to stand at a bus stop for an hour
Waiting for the government's public transport
Ignoring some overcrowded private bus
That comes every five minutes
Thumping music that can be heard
In Cuba

… Is to be fed up with waiting
(As we so often do) and jump
On one of those private buses
(You swore you'd never take again)
Only to be squashed (once more)
Like an orange being sucked
Dry of its juices

… Is to arrive at a stoplight
That has just turned green,
Cars rushing by madly
On their way to their destinations;
And yet you feel the urge
To step out in that car-mad street
Like a lunatic, cussing the cars
As if they've done you wrong
By wanting also to go their way

… Is to see a sign marked, "No Vending"
And set up a stall right under the words,
Hailing the few good –natured cops
Who will ignore the sign and wish you well;

Yet knowing when to run with your belongings
Upon hearing the distant shouts
Of “Feds! Feds!” come closer and closer.

Nemesis

She would curl herself in a fetal ball
And sleep all day in that couch in the staff lounge,
Looking as calm as a cat catching its beauty sleep.
At least, that's how I remember her best.

But there were other times when she would shout
At the top of her voice as if ready
To explode, every vein in her firm throat
Risen like snakes in a pit ready to unleash
Their venom on the next victim.

But there was one whose soothing music calmed
The beast in her; whose metabolism seemed
Immune to her stinging hisses.
And the more she tried to puncture those soft veins
The more she realized she tried in vain
To conquer this nemesis, who'd start
To play his tune that soon had her sleeping
Like a well-fed cat on his old couch.

Market Women

I honor the fat women
In large pleated skirts
Who sell in the market

They source their meat and fruits,
Vegetables and yams
With hard labor and joy

Young and old women alike
Who represent generations
Past and those to come

In that open space where
Men source the seasoning
Of their nourishment

Legend (for Michael Jackson)

This blazing sun cries
Sunlight tears
Two days after
The legend dies

A yellow butterfly
Staggers

Gray birds sing
Songs of petulant pain

An old lady curses
Her barren luck
Under a giant
Mourning mango tree

The legend is dead
But his legacy lives on
In our sorrow

Concrete Ilo

Goat skin
Wraps
The drum
In the park
The man in yellow
Beats his heart
Pounds his soul
On the auction
Blocks his mind
His own business they jump
And prance
With a crowd
At this concrete ilo

Preparing for a wrestling match of spirits.

The variety of life

A strong wind blows between the strands
Of my hair as I watch a wonderful woman
In jeans on her phone, waiting
Like I am on the bus to take us
To our separate destinations.

A white van passes by
Then a black car: the spice of life
Sweetening the air-woman and man,
Black and white; and I somewhere
Amid it all, tasting the flavor.

Sheikh

The three claw- like scars on his face
Stands royally above the raggedly shaven beard
He dons. He is in full white apparel,
Covering his jet black skin.

"I'm going to Saudi Arabia," he said,
"For Hadj (in his Nigerian accent)."
"So what title do you go by?"
I replied with an ignorant question.
"Sheikh." His tone was matter-of-fact
As if to say, *how dare you sit*
In an Religious Education meeting and not know
What 'Hadj' or 'Sheikh' are?

I smiled, saying nothing further
About the matter, feeling stupid
For having asked questions I once
Knew the answers for.

Writers' retreat

We combed the long curvature of the bay
To the point where the wall of rocks blocked us
From going around the corner where lust
Could have seeped into our hair on that day
When the sun slowly rose in the sky. The sweet spray
Of salt whetted our lips with little fuss,
The wind leaking tears from our eyes like pus
Seeping from a sore melting like wet clay.

At that point we decided to turn back
And make our way up to the bungalow
Where we stayed that weekend. Along the track
I searched to relocate my slippers so
I could continue my poetic attack
On the sea that threatens us with its flow.

Appearance versus Reality

Her question summoned the reality
That the place smelt of the stale stench
Of defecation. Then she stormed out,
Leaving me and scores of others smarting
At the smell of human excrement,
In a place that looks like a king's bedroom;
But smells more like a pauper's john!

Memories

A sudden squawk of birds
Takes flight above the deep-
Ening evening. A tree
Follows their instinctive
Action like tourists
Using little cameras
To capture scenes
The mind cannot contain.

Silence. Only the light
Of a sad sun shining
On the grass a day or two
After the birds are gone.

The stench of dog filth sweeps
In as flies swarm
Like tourists swarming scenes
In an effort to capture memories.

The darker children

I never sat on the wall at lunch time
With the fair-skinned kids-the "chiney wall"
The darker kids would call it; where the white,
Half-white, Chinese and clear-skinned Indians
Ate lunch. Instead, I stayed everywhere else
Where the 'black' kids were;
Though I didn't look much like them.
Those on the wall thought I was odd
For hanging around the darker children.
My sister herself grew one day to ask me why
I've always been drawn to our Mother's dark world,
Ignoring our father's fairer heritage.

A man lost

He slumbered by in a clown suit:
Dark jacket and flower-patterned tie;
His face rimmed with the scars
Of a life lived on the edge of guilt.

His eyes were pain
As he glanced at me, rushing by,
With his black pouch
Tucked under his arm, racing
To his ultimate purpose.
I marked his face. Saw behind the mask
And grotesque apparels, a man
Sacrificed upon the altar of his God.
A man lost in this world,
Who had found his solace somewhere
Else in a world beyond those eyes
Of pain, scarred face and mismatched clothes.

Hang time

Looking out the Open
doorway
I see the bright yellow
Sheen of the sun
Shining on the grass.

Last night a fight en-
Sued. The woman
In pink short shorts hang-
Ing out clothes opened
The door at 3 AM
And tried to hang herself
From the grill.

The fight had been going on
For some time now.
Nightly nerves fluttered
And floundered
Like a ship in a storm;
Warm currents turned cold
Stone floor
Was my bed last night
And right at that point
My head spun
When I saw her hanging from the grill like clothes.

The white apology

(I)
In Ibo culture a man is exiled
To his mother's land for committing
A female crime. He must return in shame
For seven years to that place of comfort:
His mother's bosom.

But I have returned
To my father's clan somewhere in Caribbean Europe
A cold, damp place, seeking the warmth of a man,
Neanderthal, who sleeps in caves
And hunts his food.

And yet, for all the barbarism,
I have returned to civilization in his world
In uptown St. Andrew.
(II)
Some years ago, living here, I found
The substance for "The Black Thesis"
And turned it into a master's degree.

Today, I find the source of the white apology:
A dissertation of interracial love.

Behind the line

I looked intently under the light
Of that small room for gray hairs
And could find only a few.
I guess that's why the boy asked,
"Are you Alex's brother?"
I carped out the sarcasm-
"Is it that I look that old,
Or does he look that young?"
Then, in that small room
Where bets are formalized,
I realized that he has this
Uncanny knack of sneaking
Behind the line
Like the money he owes me
Which I really don't want back.

I think of all the years
He schooled and fed me.
I realize, even though
He did that ignoble thing
Over a year ago
And went missing in the night
Without trace, when I need him
Most he's there-like some sort
Of drunk superhero, staggering
Through the night
In rescue of the desperate.

For years I've watched him
Drink smoke and curse,
Even steal a bit,
And yet he's the noblest man
I know. The golden brown of his hair,
(My sister says it's auburn blond),
The white of his skin I presume,
In this country, could get him past
Any line. But often he remains
In the darkest corners
With the blackest faces;
Smiling his sheepish smile
My female friends call "Ginal".
My male friends call him 'cool'.
I call him, "Esau, Jew, Green Flame,
Father".

Off springs

A child screams up and down the corridors.
Then rushes into a room, thoughtlessly
Pushing the door open. Smiling, I ask him
Paternal questions. He rushes out-
This mochaccino child,
Two shades darker than the French vanilla man
Who brought him here. His father is my cousin;
A light gray man like myself-
My surname behind his first.

The house, normally quiet, pants-
Tired of the usually heavy silence
And the recent darting up and down
Of feet eclectic like Man's search for identity.

The child runs outside when we step in the wide
Open world, wishing to come with us:
Two grown men reuniting after months apart-
One the offspring of the other.

To this day

The other night she revealed the great sin
She had committed at ten years old:
Her stepdad came in the room
One night when mom was out
With her other sisters. He kissed her
And fondled her in private places
Before placing in her something
So hard to this day she feels
The pushing and prodding, thrusting
And gyrating inside that delicate space
Between her bitter childhood
And emerging womanhood.

She cannot forget the guilt she felt
For telling Mother, who dismissed
Her childish lies. The beating
And cussing out she deserved for fibbing.
The stone she held thereafter,
Like a warrior princess; that, to this day,
She keeps near her bosom
For the next bwoy
Who try fi pass him place wid har;
Who must feel the guilt edge of her great sin.

Rescue

This clock ticking at my ears like my heart
Swoons me to sleep in this necropolis.

The room is raining silence like black out
While everyone inside lives in fear,

Wondering what will become of their love
Wandering aimlessly in the cold dark night.

I hear the click of fingers on keys
And turn to see a zombie-like creature,

Bald, with coarse brown skin.
The phone vibrates. The voice of love rescues.

Thunder

They wrapped himself
In the glorious garment
Of the sun,

Their bluebeards sprinkled
With the silver lining of clouds
Stalking the area.

These aging men
Danced down a storm
Under the wrinkled sky,

Singing seductive songs of Africa
In the New World.

A girl grew warm.
The sun streamed cold.
The drum hummed

Under the thunder
Of crooked fingers.

Poetics

The morning waxes poetic
The sun philosophical
Preaches wisdom as I wait
On the woman who
Over the last few months
Has caused so much sunburn
To my skin.

She holds the scorching rays
Of the sun
On her tongue's tip;
Burnt out bile in her eyes.

The sweet salt kiss of seduction on her lips.

Life in the fast lane

I sit here reading a book, contemplating
The next verse; watching women around me
Wait on men-I myself waiting on a woman.

One dashes out this morning diner, the other
Is removed by an older woman, to sit
Next to the child that resembles her.

Another woman, up in age, plays with her phone.
Then leaves in a rush, Time impending.

I consider the meeting I must have
With a woman who called me at quarter to eight,
Saying, "Meet me in an hour."

Now, long past the hour mark, I am still waiting
For this woman who I've waited on so long.

I look inside myself at the man beside me,
Looking at me, invisible in the next seat:
A man confused, who knows where to go,
Listening to the intimate conversation
Of women talking on their phones to men,
Wondering if their lives are as fast-paced.

This room

This room
Rains
In my ears
Hears
Pains my heart
Starts to ignore
My cry
For help
Helps me
Consider
My life
In a room
Where
The sound
Of a fan
Is the only
Confidante
A man
Can have

images
of a girl
in a yellow
dress
I wonder
if real
I feel
the lone-
liness
confess
the years
tears
like rain
the earth
floods
the hem-
isphere
of a room
built by gloom.

River running to the sea

We descended a trench of stone,
Passing meager, hungry dogs
And Rasta men who penetrate the air.

A bronze woman in full-bodied
Glory stood like a statue,
Shining.

Then we dug our way past
The snake roots of trees
Lurking like doom
Over the gaping sea
Before entering the ice waters
Below.

The river roared
Over rigid rocks
Creating a cavity
Inside the great wall
Where lovers hid
Their passion like treasures
Hidden in secret places
Of this Caribbean dream.

The yearning sea below,
The imposing river above
The communal bath
Of friends and acquaintances

And with me, one who
Handed me soap
So I could refresh my empty emotions.

Winged insect

On the back page of a book, as I write
A poem about aging beauty, a fragile
Little winged insect pitches and stays still
For quite a while. I try to close the book
But can't bring myself to crush
This white-coated friend, no bigger than a rice grain.

He moves about in circles
But never flies away, bringing me to consider
How I can close my book without injuring
This creature that seems to have taken a liking
To my words. So after much deliberation
I blow it away with one cold breath
On an otherwise hot night.

Philosophy lesson

I met her once- a dazzling beauty
I proclaimed-somewhere past the Middle Ages.

I thought of her yesterday as I taught
About the Dark Ages when superstition ruled,

Trying myself to peep into that darker world
Where absolute truth exists.

The classroom was light in a dark night of searching
Beyond question-less faces that seem bent

By the need to swallow someone else's thoughts
Then regurgitate them like vomit.

Transformation

It seems only when her counterpart,
Weird sister number one, appears
She transforms into a Christian witch:
Obese bearded man-woman
Who lives within an earshot next door,
Who speaks the language of clamor.
Fingers crooked like the branches
Of a Christ-cursed tree bearing no fruit.
Eyes beaming like a demon's.
Dressed in black apparel, cone-shaped hat
And the aura of magic.

But when she is away from the barren one,
She becomes an angel.
The white gloss of her robes outlines
Her slender voice, her voice
Piercing the dark with its subtle radiance
And mystic splendor that lightens the air.

Charlie

(I)

Would stand
And watch

Us laugh
And talk

Reporting everything
We said

In the present tense
As if

He was living his life
Through us

(II)

Often we'd see him going
The other way

At nights as we strolled
To a party

And we'd see him again
As we returned

In the demon hours
Of the night

Smiling an angelic glow
As he glided by us

As if guiding us
From that other side

(III)

One day we heard
In his sleep he died

We went to his house
After that and saw

Paintings drawings
Masterpieces of his creation

(IV)

Later on, we discovered that his wife
Had left him years before and took
The kids with her to a foreign country
Leaving him a man stuck in a time warp
Where the past is ever replaying in the present.

Afternoon sleep

The air is still
This afternoon
As the sun's scorch
Creates a bleached screen
Before the mountains
Fading in the parched brightness
Of this dry white season.

The tropics have become
Winter in summer,
Snowing sun rays in white droplets
Of fire. Desire rests,
Dreaming of fidelity
In a dishonest bed.

Fat fleas creep
From bodies
That have come
In contact with germs
From a third party,
Drinking stimulants
With a woman
Who sleeps,
Body contorted
By her own smeared conscience.

Proficiency Test I

The atmosphere is serene
Here inside
This college cave where
The scene
Is silence

Violence
Penetrates
The air
After the "zeen"
Irritates
The ears
Of those who stood
At the divide
Between Man's
Commercial cares
And The Good.

Proficiency Test II

The exam began a few minutes past nine
In the large Assembly Hall, people filing in
All and sundry, for half an hour. like slaves,
The place abuzz. Until, finally the mood
Fell calm for the next few hours
As lowered heads concentrated
On the task at hand:
Writing an exam to matriculate in
The University of the West Indies,
That 'free place of learning' built upon
An old sugar plantation.

Devil's advocate

Her wailing words played devil's advocate
With my mind, tempting me to believe
Her lies. I stood at the highest point
Overlooking the world, without realizing
That it was all an illusion:
That I was really battling demons
Of my own mistakes.

It's a hard thing to be haunted by one's sins
But unbearable to fight someone else's;
Whether atop the highest hill
Or sinking in the lowest valleys of this world.

A half-brother could be a secret lover;
A lover a hatred adversary,
Being led to the point of elimination
Against the high winds of deception
Or the gut-wrenching fall of revelation.

Evil fairy

This woman beside me
Is a witch, conjuring
A wall of resistance
From the book of spells
She reads
To summon untruths.

I inspect the contours
Of her fairy tale face;
The evil of her empty eyes
Like the wicked witch
In a tale of envy
Where beauty is slain
By one sinister look.

Her smile

She smiled at every insult he dished out
From across that well-kept room up that hill
Where he lived and taught poetry
For a living. But he couldn't understand
Her nonchalant disregard for his reverse psycho-
Logy: how he said such hurtful things
To inspire her to do better, because,
As he claimed, "She was not pulling her weight
In the workshop". She remained as stark as death.

I watched her head hang low as if in shame.
Then rise with a grimace,
Mistaken for a recalcitrant smile
Like the defiant resurrection of Christ.

I realized his agnostic ignorance
To the nature of the human spirit.
"It's not that she's not moved
By your criticism, Sir, but rather
That she's hiding her remorse
Behind a painted smile." I declared.

She nodded, acknowledging the terrible truth
Of the statement, leading him
To proclaim me a poet in a room
Full of poets, like himself, who couldn't see
The hidden language of hurt
Behind her stark smile.

River song I

The road
To the river
Is a long
Windy road
Laced with rocks
And, as the female
Child says,
"A trench full
A deep"
That cascades
Past goats
Eating grass
In the bushes
To the side
Until
A small stream
Cross sections
The path where
Stones
Wet
With orgasm
Break
The small waters
Of tributaries
Hiding behind
Bushes and slopes
Dancing into woods
Mythologizing

Family outings
Creolizing
Classical myth
With Jamaican
Folklore

The path whines up-
Wards into avenues
Of childhood memories
With children
In the present
Running at the edge
Of steep cliffs
Overhanging
Forgotten valleys
Where spirits howl
Like wolves

Lying listening

(I)

Last night
Three birds
In their cages
Scratching

I lied
There
Listening
To their irritation

(II)

This morning
Students
In an exam
Writing

I sit
Here
Listening
To their concentration.

The river's mouth

We went down to the river's mouth
Via the long descending track
Lying deep in trenches of stone
Past goats grazing as silent as lambs
To the slaughter in bushes along the byway.

We soon encountered a little stream
Where waters serenely rest,
Calling for someone to lather
In its purity.
"This is not the river." The five year-old boy
Instructed. Earlier his grandmother had said,
"Follow your nose".
We rose up
A steep hill where a track
As narrow as vines curled
Like a snake slithering to strike;
Leading to a plateau of voices
Bellowing like maroon warriors
Ready for battle.
By then the women
And female child had caught up
With our enterprise, directing us
To a makeshift pool where
Breasts hung
Like vines from flatulating bamboos
Overhead.
We dived in and watched
Those melons being rubbed in circles

As we circulated like blood
Around the body,
The mouth opening
To let us in; the boy scared
Of entering its gaping hole.

Scorpion

Of love
Stinging my heart
With the poison
Of your late October lies

My eyes
Hypnotize
To your mesmerizing stare

Dark affinities
Possess
My being
With inertia

Your tail curls
Over my resistance

I paralyze

In your eyes

Await
Sting

Probe
Your stance

And prepare
To meet

Infinity.

www.ingramcontent.com/pod-product-compliance
Lightning Source LLC
Chambersburg PA
CBHW022200160726
48282CB00024B/267
* 9 7 8 8 1 1 9 6 5 4 5 9 8 *